a gift for:

....

from:

....

ANDY GRIFFITH

The CHRISTMAS GUEST

BASED ON "THE CHRISTMAS GUEST"
A Song by Louis M. (Grandpa) Jones and Bill Walker

AND "WHERE LOVE IS, GOD IS"
A Short Story by Leo Tolstoy

Nashville, Tennessee

THIS IS MY COMMANDMENT,

THAT YOU LOVE ONE ANOTHER

AS I HAVE LOVED YOU.

—JOHN 15:12

TRADITIONS ARE IMPORTANT TO INDIVIDUALS AND FAMILIES AS CHRISTMAS APPROACHES, A TIME OF JOY TO CELEBRATE THE BIRTH OF OUR SAVIOR JESUS CHRIST. WORSHIP IN CHURCH THROUGH MUSIC IS REALLY THE ONLY TRADITION THAT HAS REMAINED WITH ME ALL 77 YEARS OF MY LIFE.

———————— ❦ ————————

As a boy, I remember carrying my trombone walking four miles with my father through cold, slippery ice to play at our church only to arrive there and see the sign "Services Canceled". Daddy and I were not upset. We enjoyed each other's company and merely turned around to walk home.

A decade or so ago, my wife, Cindi, and I were working on a television show in California and had to work until late Christmas Eve. People in the higher management roles of the show had planned an elaborate party with gourmet food and everything and insisted we be their guests. I explained that Cindi and I were going to church. Our would–be hosts could not accept that, but our plans for church won the decision. And we received a most special gift during that service: An older man played "I'll Be Home for Christmas" on his trombone. I thought he must have been with one of the big bands during their magnificent time, for he was the best musician I had ever heard. We left the church holding a single candle singing "Silent Night" and knowing it was our best Christmas ever.

Cindi and I spent all the following Christmas holidays quietly in North Carolina very happy with our home, music, and worship activities. Then, in 2002 we were invited to some friends' fiftieth wedding anniversary in Hawaii. We were hesitant to change what had become our Christmas tradition, but thought how enjoyable it would be to hear a grand choir sing at midnight services in California and planned our schedule accordingly. We had a jam-packed holiday planned when, still in North Carolina, I found myself talking by telephone to my old friend Aaron Ruben, a creator of *The Andy Griffith Show*. We were saying we wished we could see one another again, but my holiday schedule was so full. And then I realized, I had Christmas Day in Los Angeles open. We had not scheduled anything on that day in order to rest and quietly worship.

On December 25, 2002, Cindi and I were the guests of Aaron and Maureen Ruben, along with Don Knotts and Francy Yarborough, for a most special afternoon of sharing memories. It was a simple occasion during which the six of us expressed our continuing love for one another.

It has been a blessing to have the opportunity to record "The Christmas Guest," written by Louis M. Jones and Bill Walker. Grandpa Jones was a unique storyteller and is legendary among musicians, such as those who recorded this timeless story along with me.

May you feel the love of Jesus Christ and share His goodness with others every day of your life.

Merry Christmas! *Andy Griffith*

BE HOSPITABLE TO ONE ANOTHER

WITHOUT GRUMBLING. AS EACH ONE

HAS RECEIVED A GIFT, MINISTER IT

TO ONE ANOTHER, AS GOOD STEWARDS

OF THE MANIFOLD GRACE OF GOD.

—1 PETER 4:9–10

It happened one day near December's end

Two neighbors called on an old-time friend

And they found his shop so meager and lean

Made gay with a thousand boughs of green.

And Conrad was sitting with face a'shined

When he suddenly stopped as he stitched a twine

And he said: "Old friends at dawn today

When the cock was crowing the night away

The Lord appeared in a dream to me

And said 'I am coming your Guest to be'

So I've been busy with feet astir

And strewing my shop with branches of fir.

"The table is spread and the kettle is shined

And over the rafters the holly is twined.

And now I'll wait for my Lord to appear

And listen closely so I will hear His step

As He nears my humble place

And I open the door and look on His face."

So his friends went home and left Conrad alone

For this was the happiest day he had known.

For long since his family had passed away

And Conrad had spent many a sad Christmas Day

But he knew with the Lord as his Christmas Guest

This Christmas would be the dearest and best.

He listened with only joy in his heart

And with every sound he would rise with a start

And look for the Lord to be at his door

Like the vision he had a few hours before.

THE ORDINARY ACTS WE PRACTICE

EVERY DAY AT HOME ARE OF MORE

IMPORTANCE TO THE SOUL THAN

THEIR SIMPLICITY MIGHT SUGGEST.

—THOMAS MOORE

HE HEALS THE

BROKENHEARTED

AND BINDS UP

THEIR WOUNDS.

—PSALM 147:3

So he ran to the window after hearing a sound

But all he could see on the snow-covered ground

Was a shabby beggar whose shoes were torn,

And all of his clothes were ragged and worn.

But Conrad was touched and he went to the door,

And he said, "Your feet must be frozen and sore.

I have some shoes in my shop for you

And a coat that will keep you warmer too."

So with grateful heart, the man went away,

But Conrad noticed the time of day.

He wondered what made the Lord so late

And how much longer he'd have to wait.

When he heard a knock he ran to the door,

But it was only a stranger once more,

A bent old lady with a shawl of black

With a bundle of kindling piled on her back.

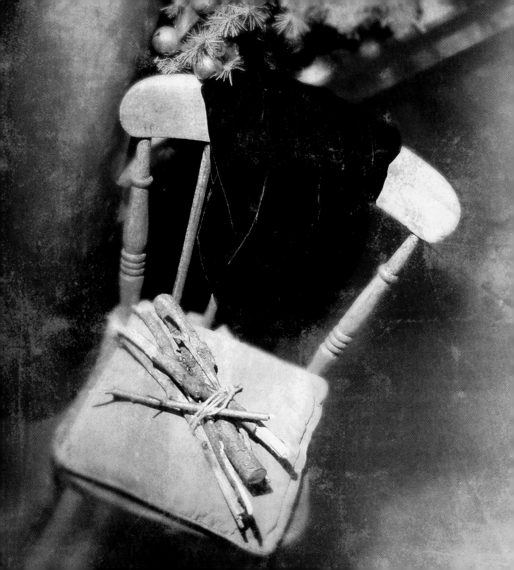

*S*he asked for only a place to rest,

But that was reserved for Conrad's great Guest.

But her voice seemed to plead "Don't send me away;

Let me rest for awhile on Christmas Day."

So Conrad brewed her a steaming cup

And told her to sit at the table and sup.

But after she left he was filled with dismay

For he saw that the hours were slipping away.

And the Lord hadn't come as He said He would,

And Conrad felt sure he had misunderstood

When out of the stillness he heard a cry,

"Please help me, and tell me where am I!"

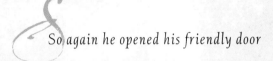So again he opened his friendly door

And stood disappointed as twice before.

It was only a child who had wandered away

And was lost from her family on Christmas Day.

Again Conrad's heart was heavy and sad,

But he knew he should make the little girl glad.

So he called her in and wiped her tears

And quieted all her childish fears.

Then he led her back to her home once more,

But as he entered his own darkened door

He knew that the Lord was not coming today

For the hours of Christmas had passed away.

So he went to his room and knelt down to pray,

And he said: "Dear Lord, why did You delay?

What kept You from coming to call on me?

For I wanted so much Your face to see."

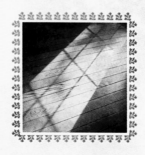

When soft in the silence, a voice he heard:

"Lift up your head, for I kept My word.

Three times My shadow crossed your floor.

Three times I came to your lowly door.

TO GENEROUS SOULS

EVERY TASK IS NOBLE.

—EURIPIDES

BE KINDLY AFFECTIONATE TO ONE ANOTHER WITH BROTHERLY LOVE, IN HONOR GIVING PREFERENCE TO ONE ANOTHER; NOT LAGGING IN DILIGENCE, FERVENT IN SPIRIT, SERVING THE LORD; REJOICING IN HOPE, PATIENT IN TRIBULATION, CONTINUING STEADFASTLY IN PRAYER; DISTRIBUTING TO THE NEEDS OF THE SAINTS, GIVEN TO HOSPITALITY.

—ROMANS 12:10-13

"For I was the beggar with bruised, cold feet.

I was the woman you gave something to eat.

And I was the child on the homeless street.

"Three times I knocked; three times I came in,

And each time I found the warmth of a friend.

Of all the gifts love is the best

I was honored to be your Christmas Guest."

ONE NEEDS A NEIGHBOR

ON WHOM TO PRACTICE COMPASSION.

—PHYLLIS McGINLEY

Then the righteous will answer Him, saying, "Lord, when did we see You hungry and feed You, or thirsty and give You drink? When did we see You a stranger and take You in, or naked and clothe You? Or when did we see You sick, or in prison, and come to You?" And the King will answer and say to them, "Assuredly, I say to you, inasmuch as you did it to one of the least of these My brethren, you did it to Me."

—Matthew 25:37-40

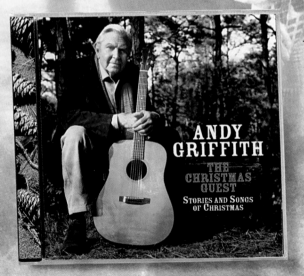

The perfect companion to this book, Andy Griffith's *The Christmas Guest* is a new collection of holiday stories and songs to celebrate the season. Produced by Marty Stuart, *The Christmas Guest* is sure to become a quintessential family holiday classic for years to come.